NATIONAL GEOGRAPHIC

T0042291

Who Lives at the Zoo?

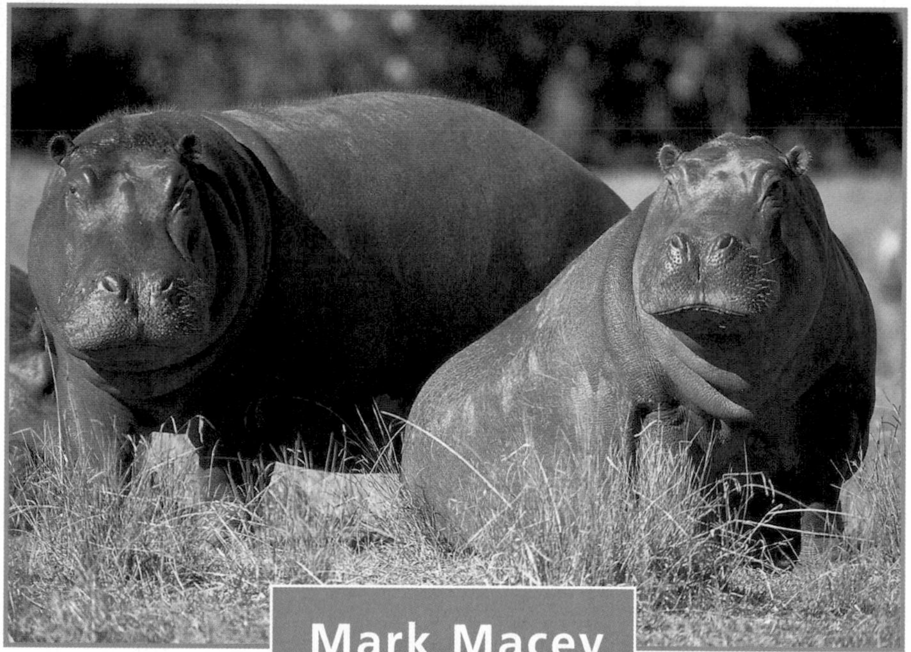

Mark Macey

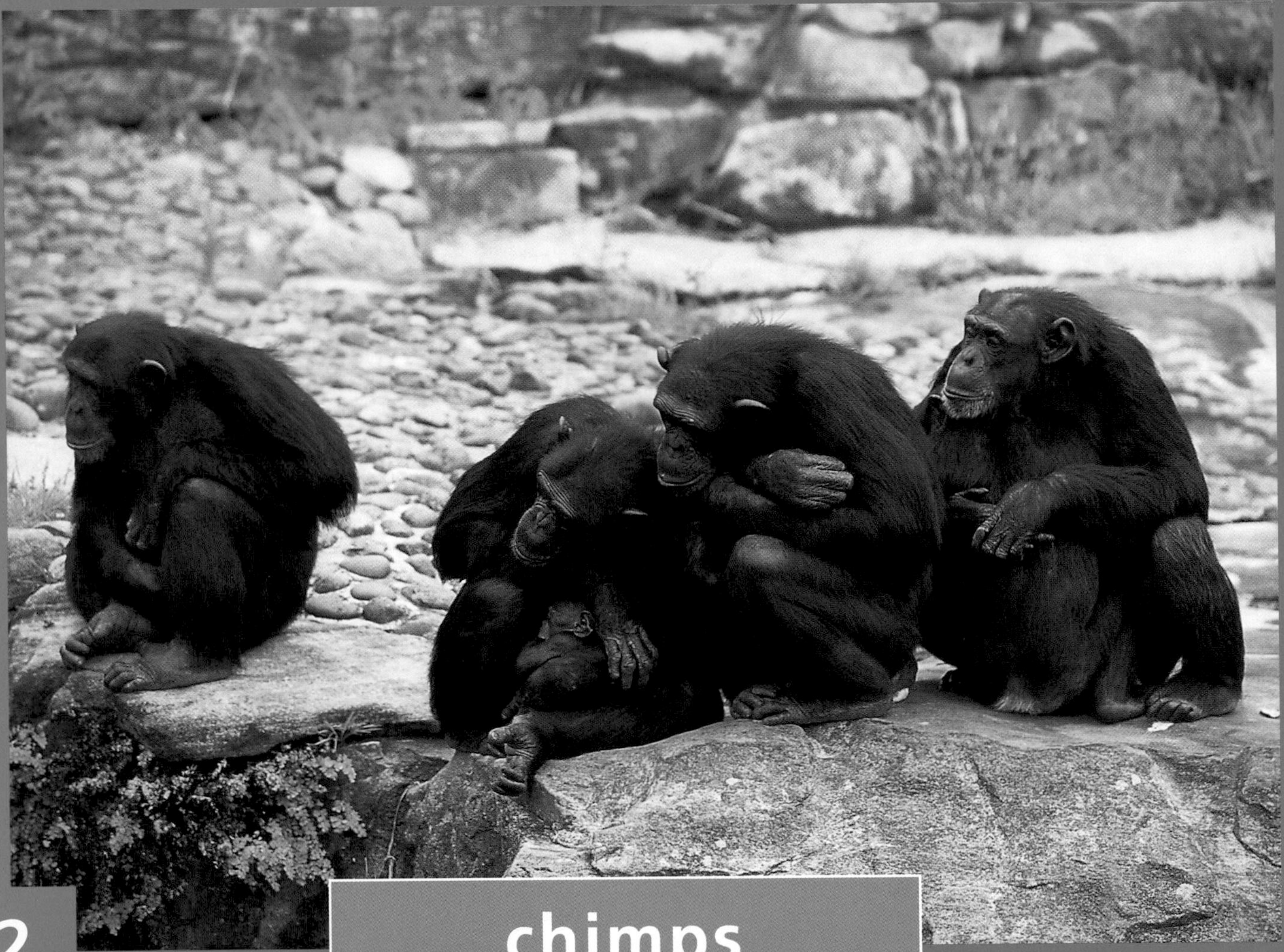

chimps

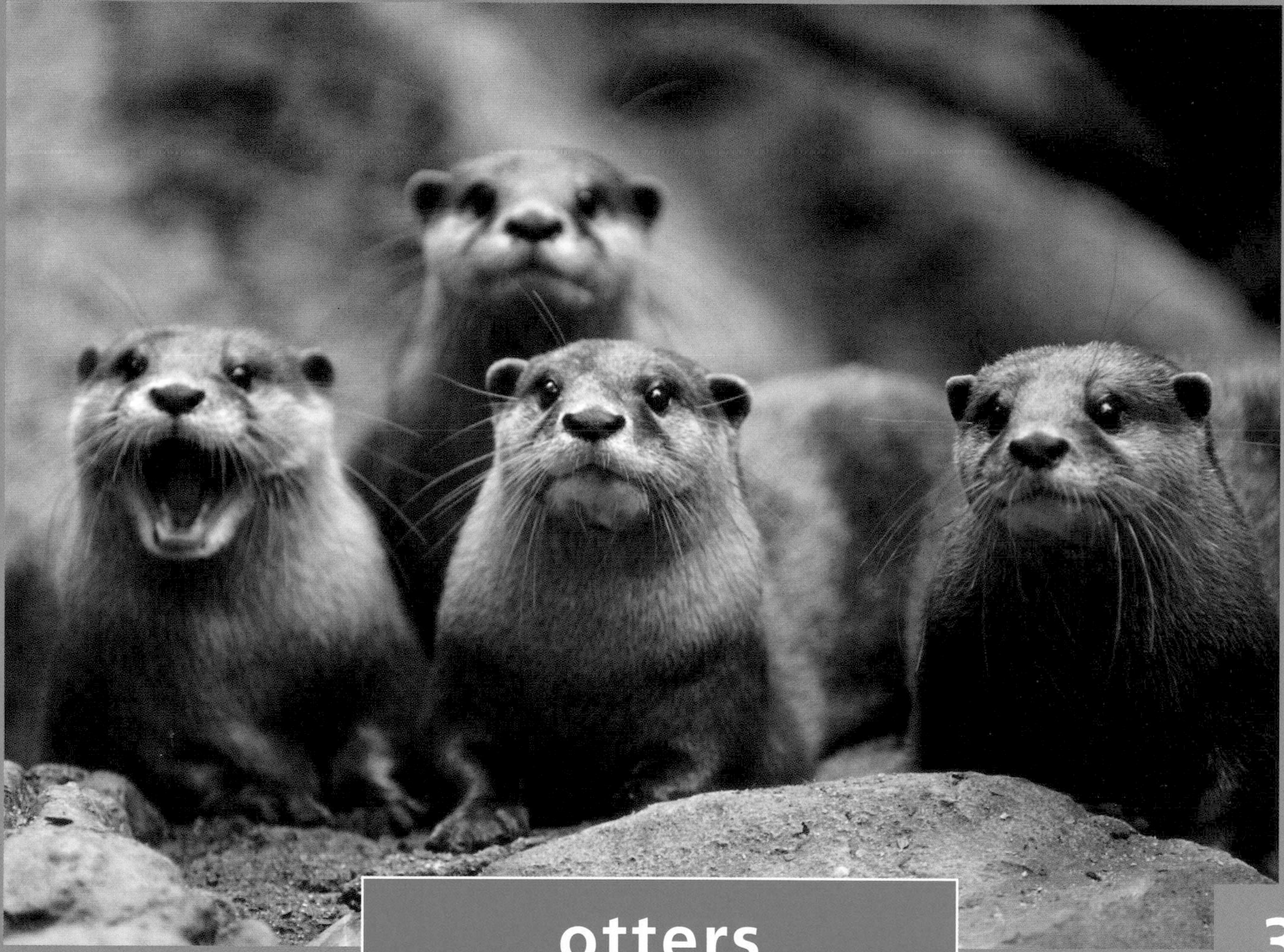

otters

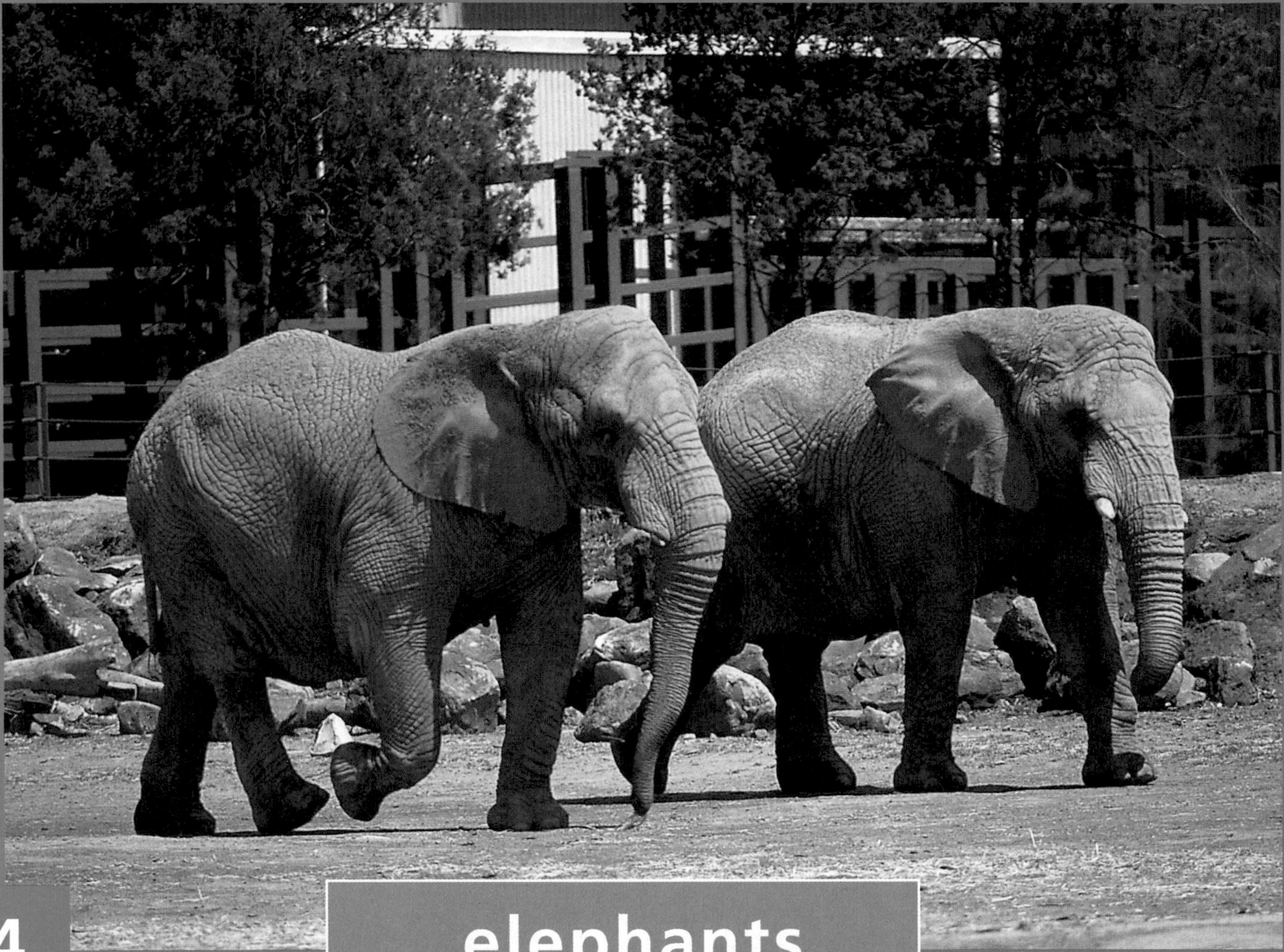

elephants

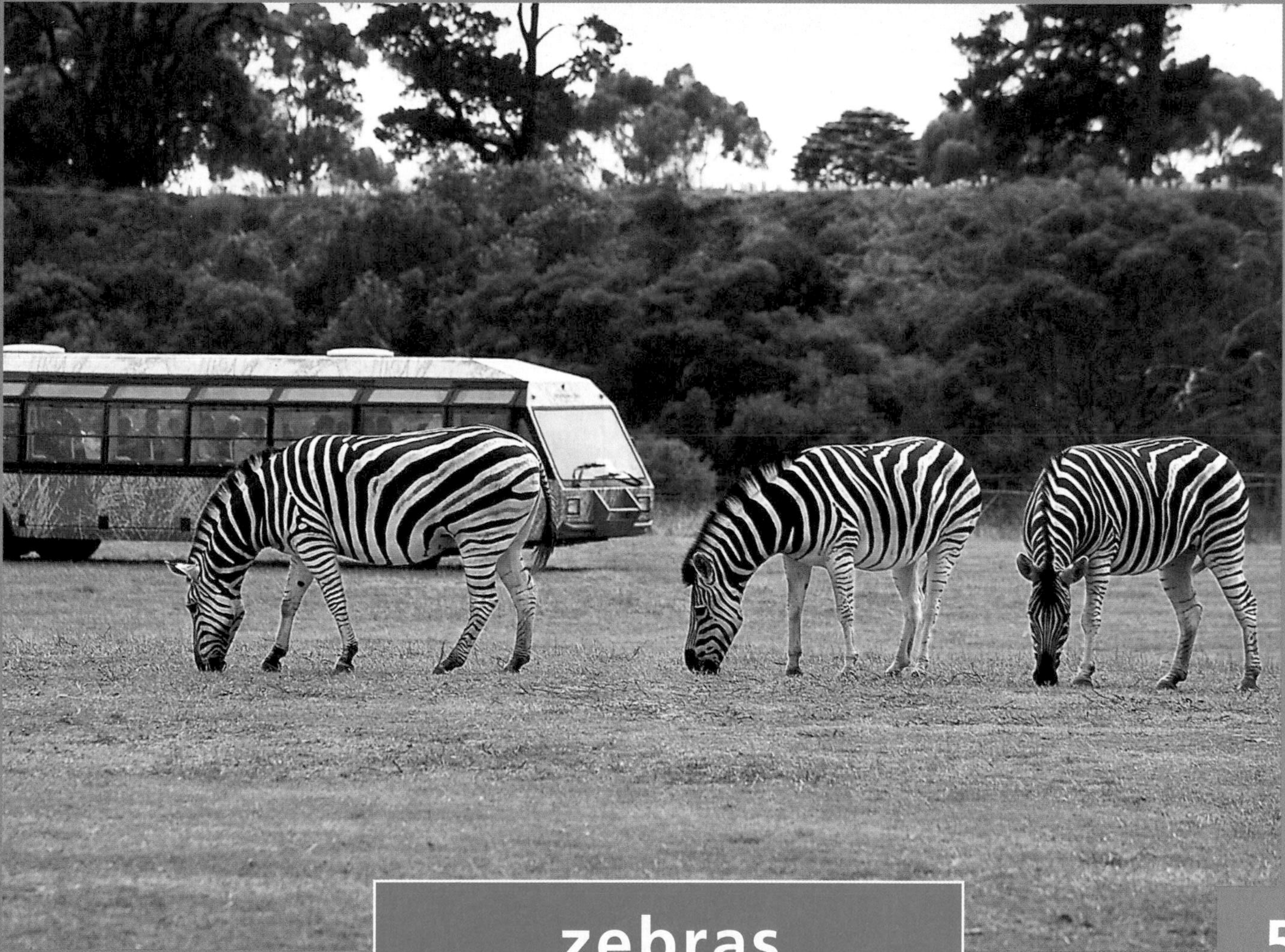

zebras

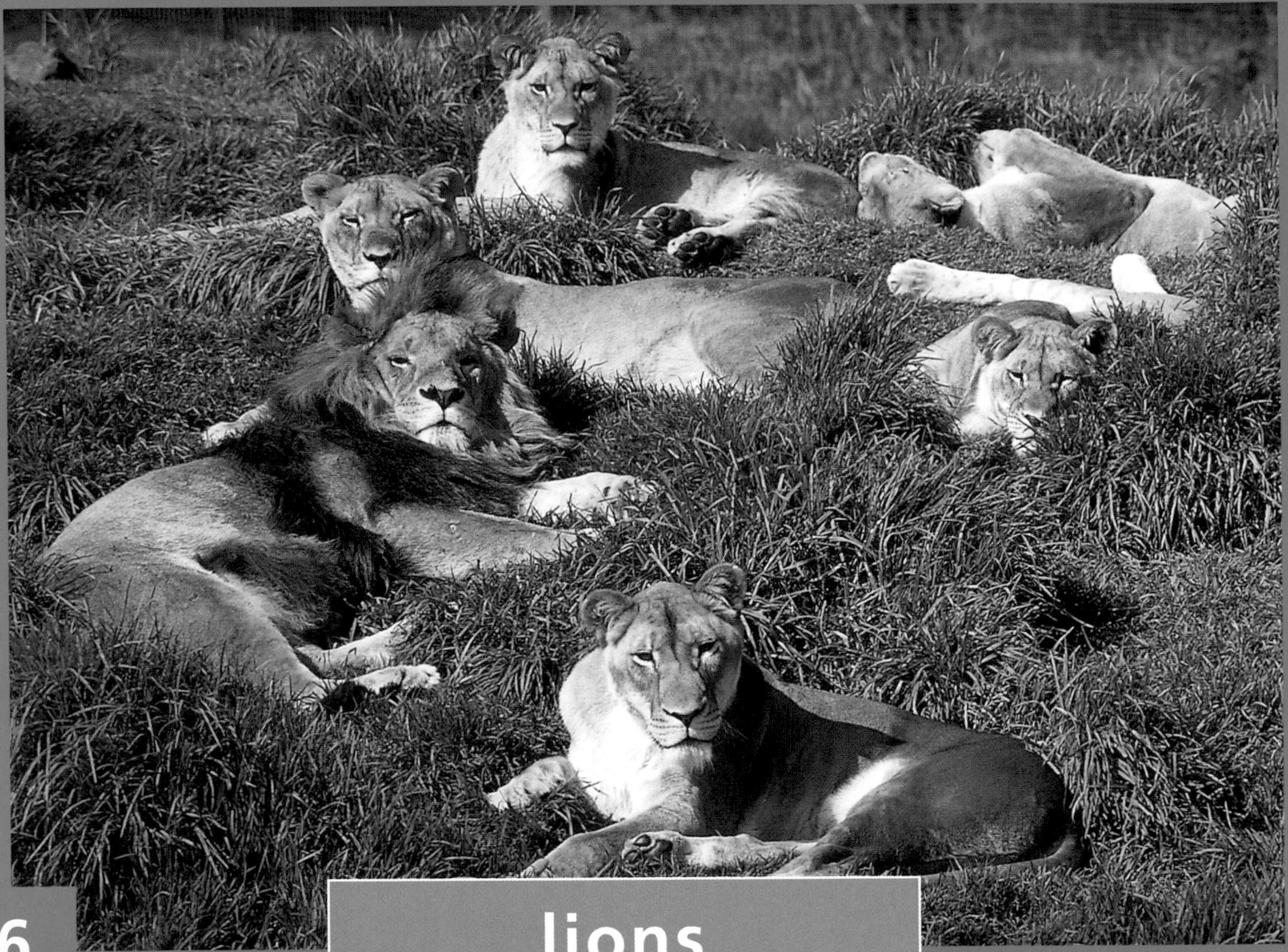

lions

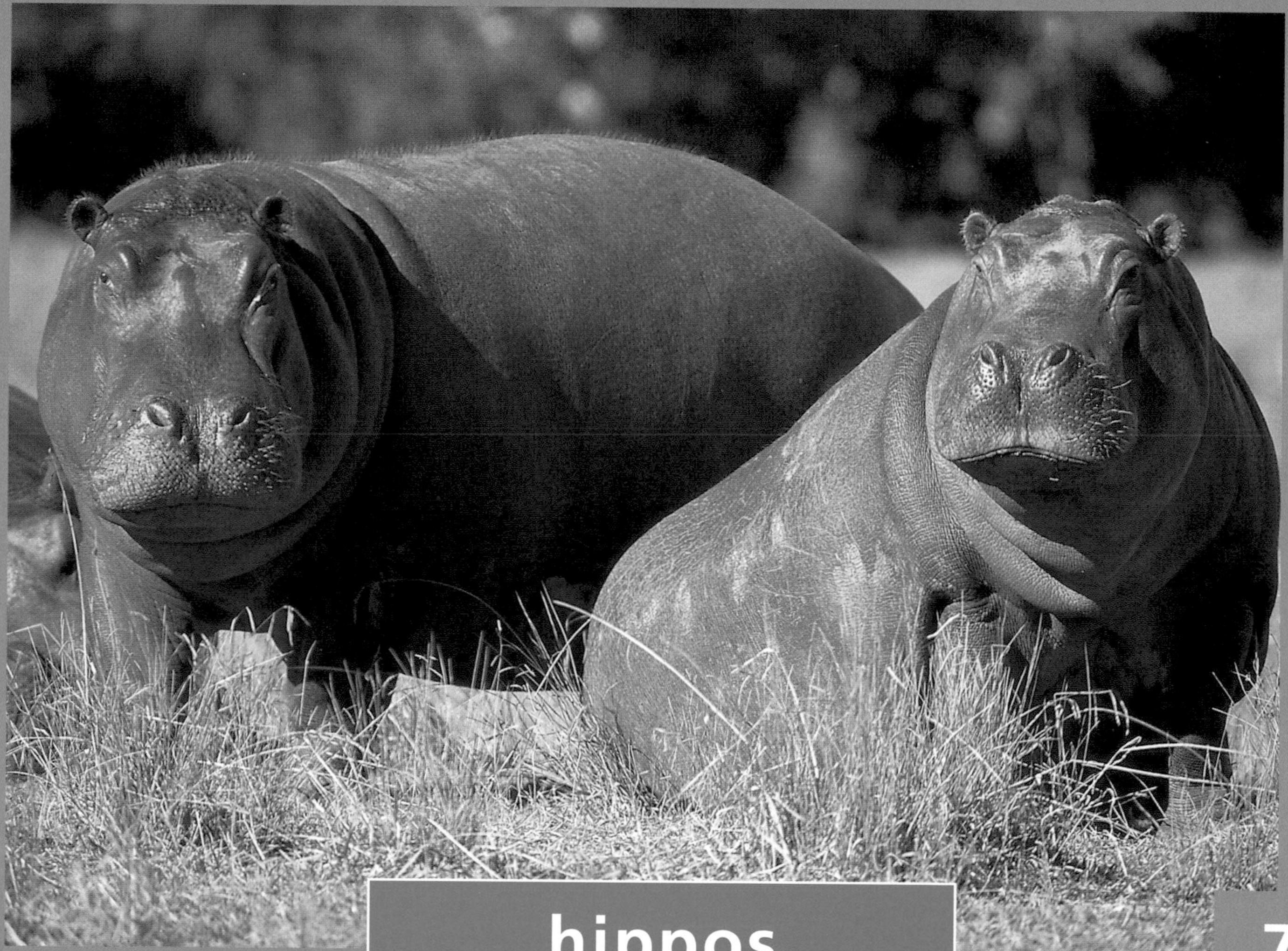

hippos

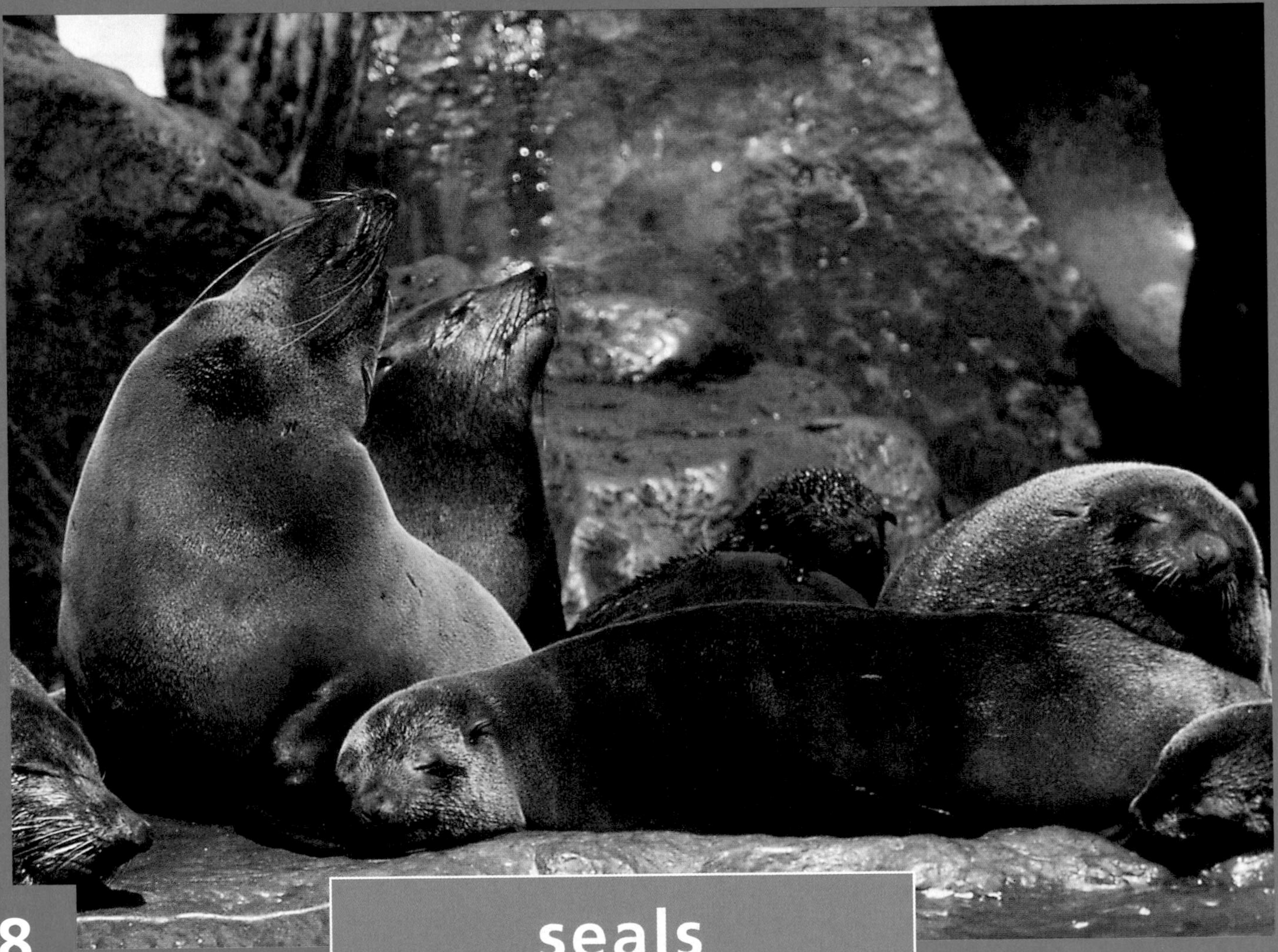

seals

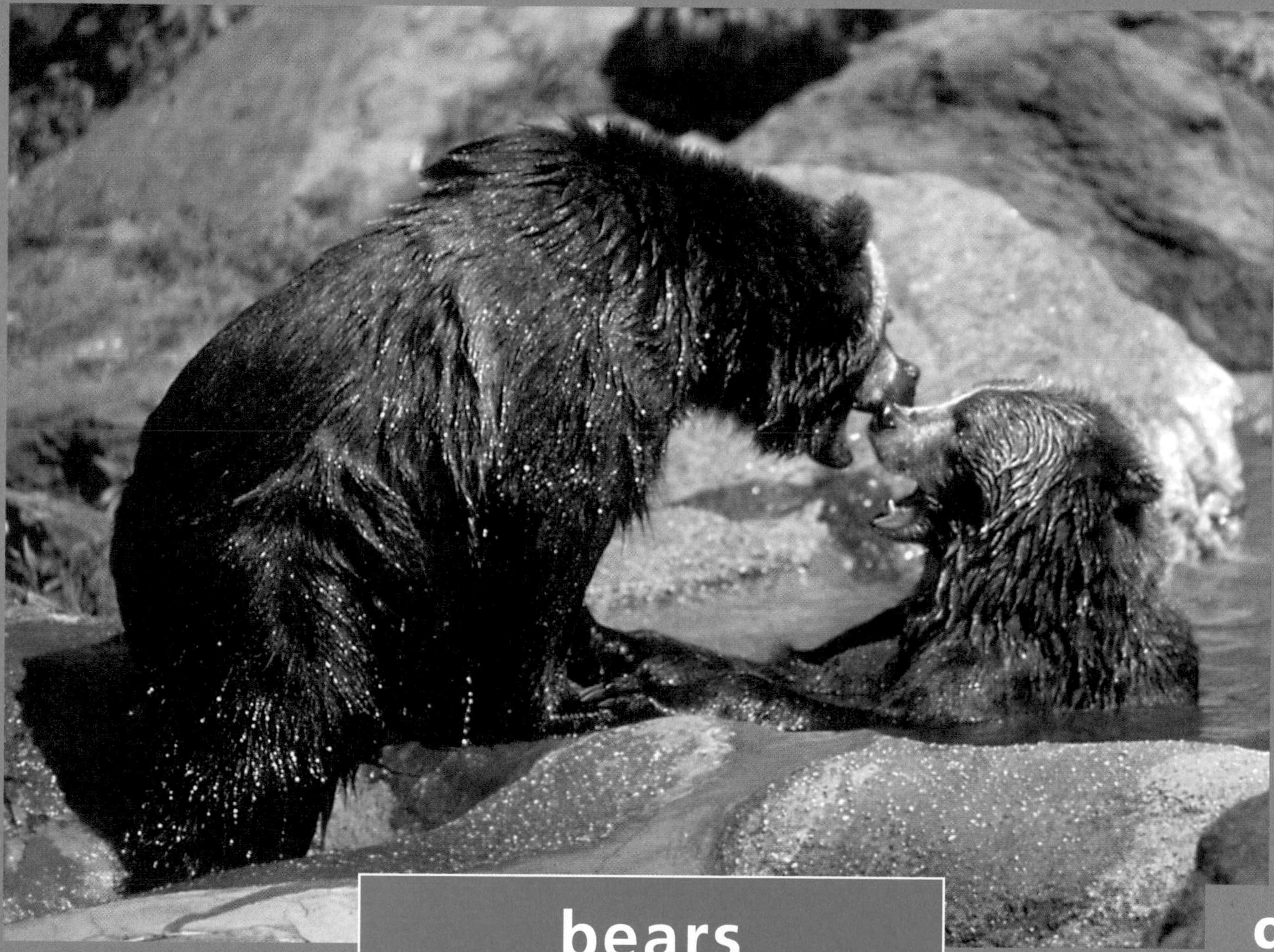

bears

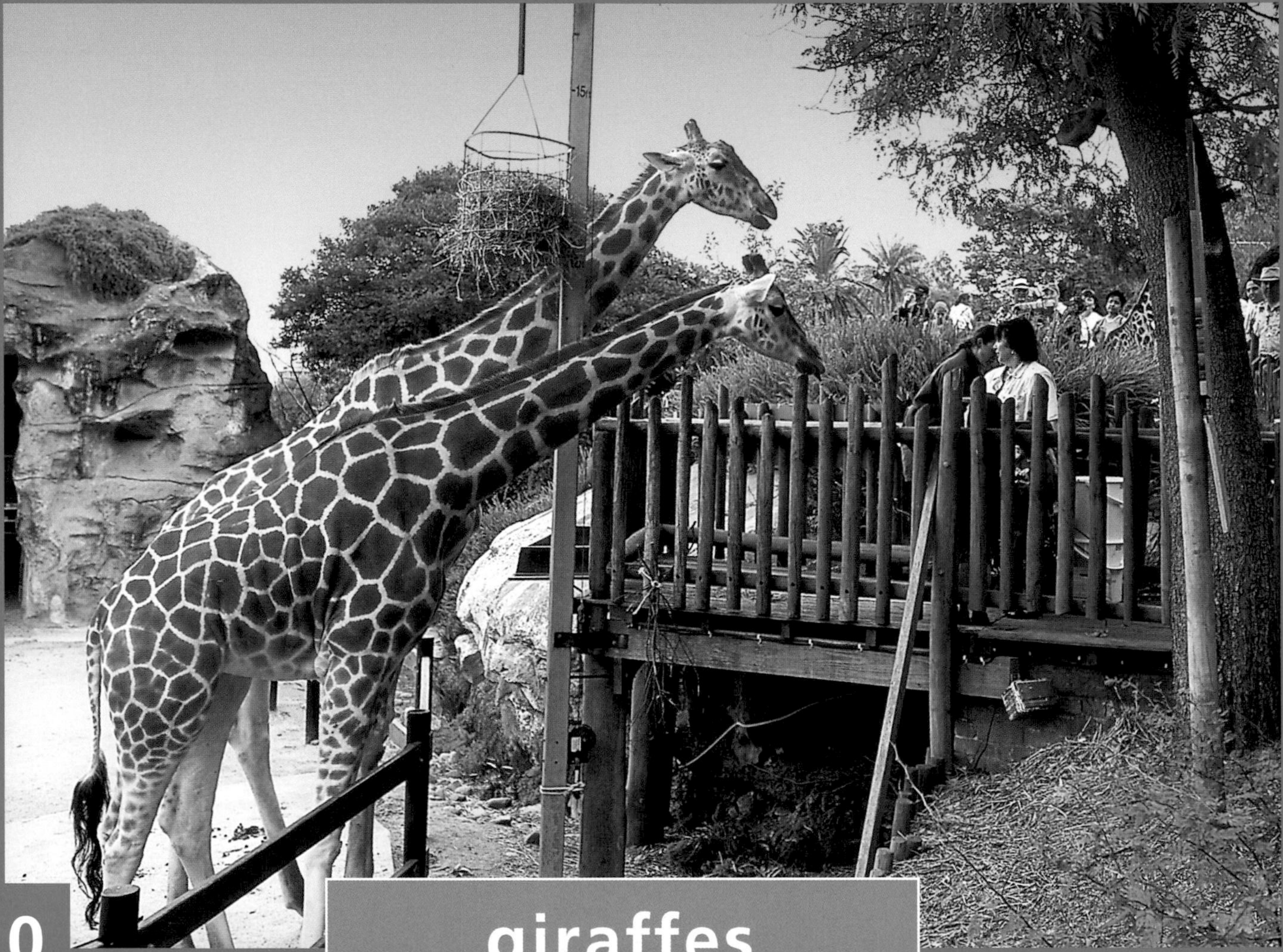

giraffes

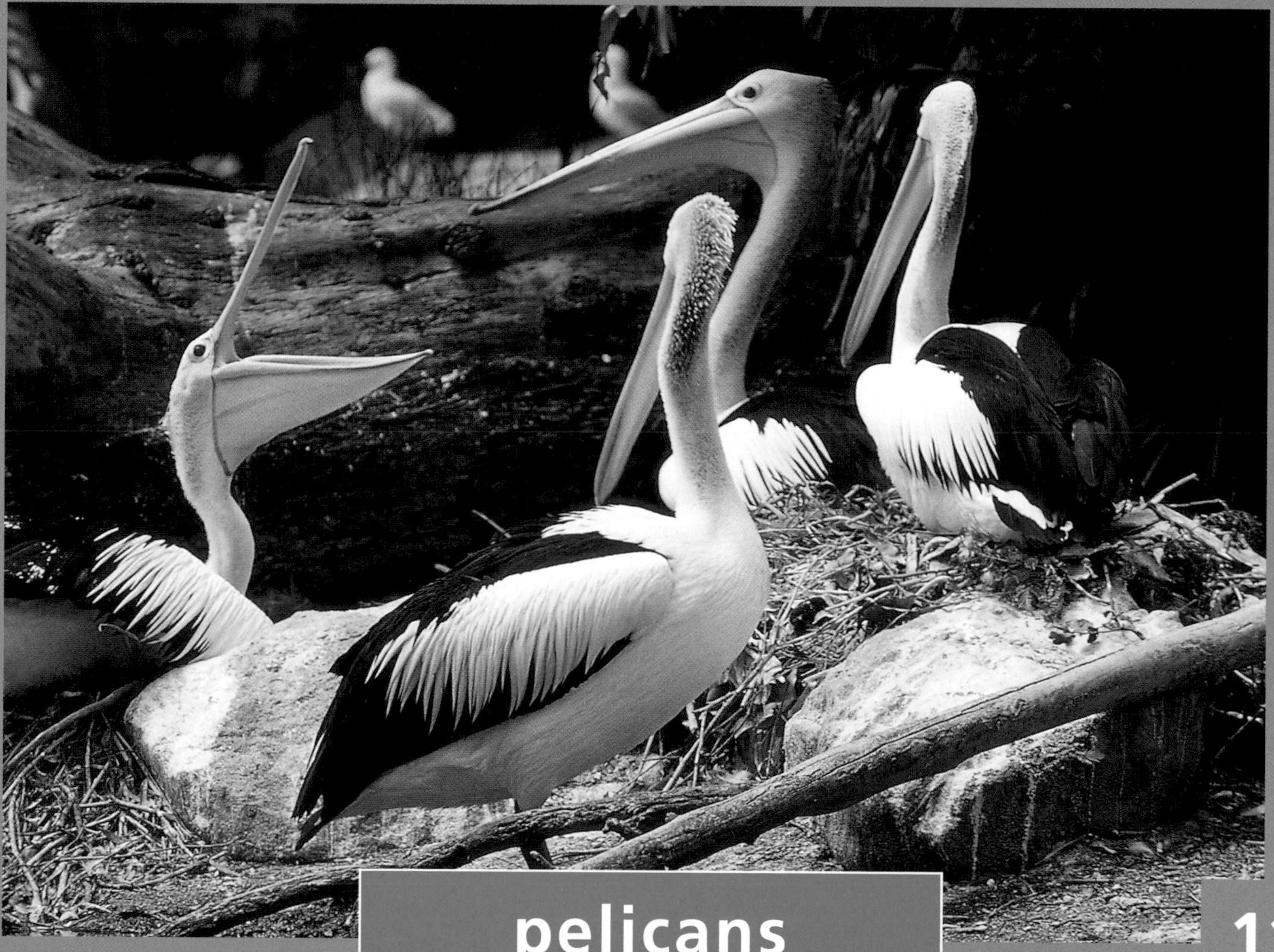

pelicans

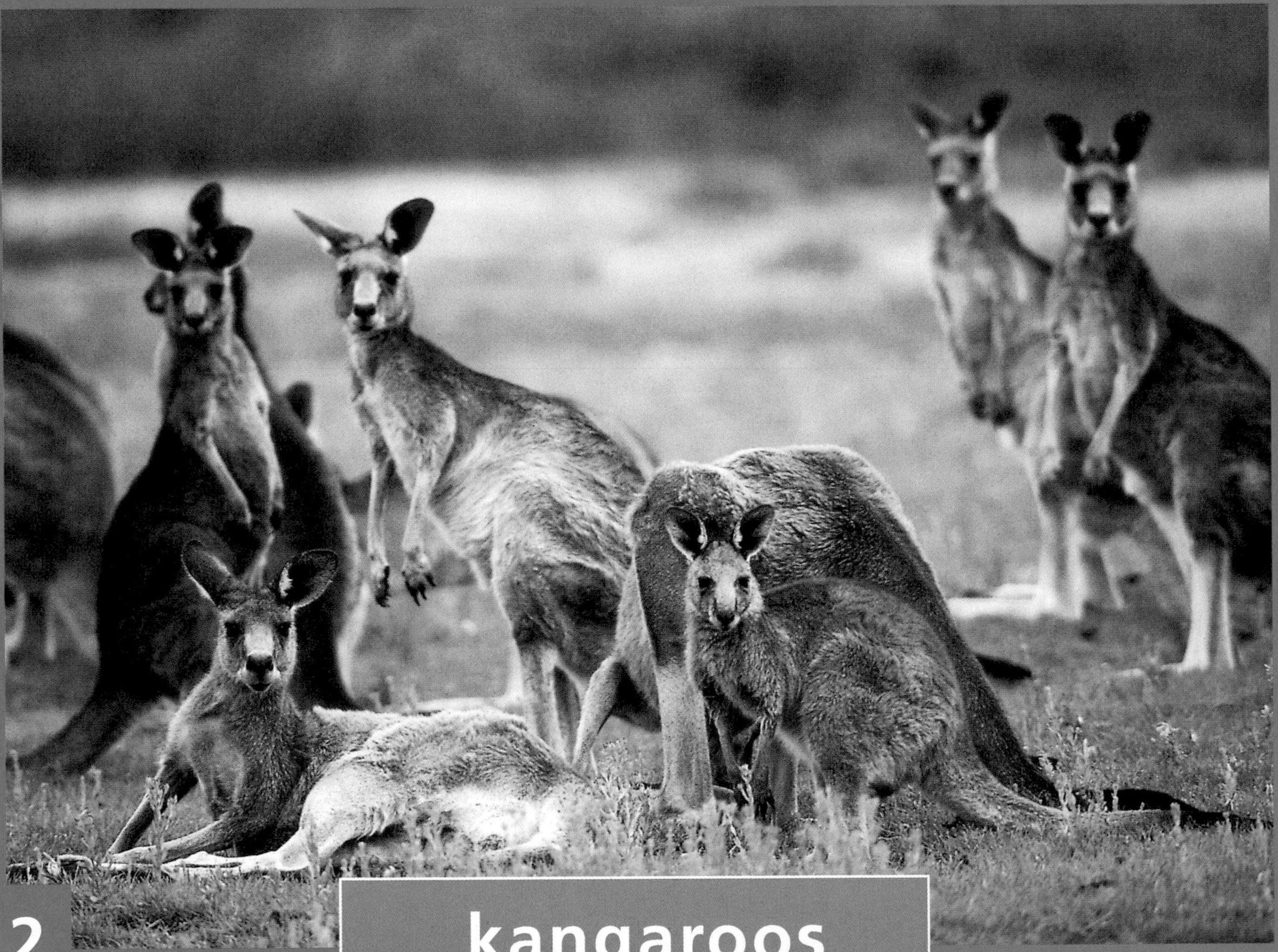

kangaroos